THE
FAMILY'S GUIDE
TO YOUR FUNERAL PLAN

Just the way you would like it, your final wishes for the end of life: well-executed, no guessing, nothing forgotten in the celebration of your life so the family's grief is made easy!

JENNI BLAIR

ABOUT THE AUTHOR

JENNI BLAIR has a passion and a zest for life, communication, and adventure. Born in New Zealand in the 1960s, she has lived in England, Iceland, Spain and Russia. She and her Kiwi husband, Duncan, met in London; after nine years of property development and a senior role in the corporate sector, they bought an A-class Burstner motorhome and travelled Europe and the British Isles for two and a half years. On returning to NZ, Jenni set up and ran two businesses, a rental and an Airbnb management company, and sold them in 2021. Over Jenni's career, she has owned six companies and spent 14 years in senior management recruitment for Wellington and London companies. In her earlier career, she loved the hospitality industry, where she managed a large hotel in the '80s, two restaurants and a French bakery, turning all into thriving businesses.

She is now semi-retired, living in an A-Class Dethleffs motorhome and has been travelling around New Zealand for the past three years.

With a never-ending energy for growth and self-worth, she writes self-help books with humour and authenticity. Her motto is, "You only have one life, so make it count; surround yourself with people whose company you enjoy and who make you laugh."

TABLE OF CONTENTS

INTRODUCTION

Let's face it, we are all going to die!

At 25, getting into a car accident is tragic and unexpected. At 46, battling leukemia as a mother of three is devastating. At 62 while cooking dinner, suddenly, you're gone. At 78, you've reached the average age for a New Zealand man. And at 97, well, you might just be ready.

But here's the million-dollar question: Will your final bash be a perfect reflection of you, or a well-meaning mess?

Why leave your loved ones scrambling to pull together your life's celebration with only a couple of days when you can plan your epic send-off now?

Ready to script your grand finale? Buckle up, friend. We're about to make death the liveliest topic in town!

Throughout the book, I've provided spaces for you to jot down your immediate thoughts. Once you've had time to reflect, visit the website at the end of the book to access an activity sheet to create your personalized funeral plan.

CHAPTER 1:

Understanding the Importance of Funeral Planning

Why is funeral planning important?

Picture this: You're gone. Poof. Your family's huddled around a table, red-eyed and shell-shocked, trying to piece together your life story and final wishes. They're arguing over whether you'd prefer roses or lilies, unsure if you wanted to be buried or scattered to the four winds. It's a nightmare but an unfortunate reality even right now for families across the world.

But it doesn't have to be this way.

Funeral planning isn't just about picking out a fancy box or deciding between "Amazing Grace" and "Stairway to Heaven." It's your last love letter to the world, your ultimate "I've got this" to the people you're leaving behind.

You plan birthdays, weddings, vacations. So why not your grand exit? It's the one party you're guaranteed not to attend, but boy, can you make it unforgettable.

Here's the cold, hard truth: Death doesn't check your calendar. It doesn't care if you're 25 or 95, if you've climbed Everest or barely made it up your driveway. It's the great equalizer, the one appointment we all keep.

So why leave your final story in someone else's hands?

By planning your funeral, you're not being morbid – you're being mighty. You're taking control, easing burdens, and ensuring your life is celebrated exactly as how you lived it. No more guessing games, no more family feuds over your favorite hymn.

But it's more than just logistics. It's about legacy. It's about turning your funeral from a somber affair into a powerful tribute that echoes long after the last guest has left. It's about giving your loved ones the gift of clarity in their darkest hour, allowing them to grieve without the added stress of decision-making.

Then, there's the issue of money. Funerals can be expensive – shockingly so. By planning ahead, you save your family from emotional turmoil (and potentially saving them) from financial ruin. It's like buying insurance, but instead of protecting your family against accidents, you're safeguarding their peace of mind.

Remember, this isn't about dwelling on death – it's about celebrating life. Your life. In all its messy, beautiful and unique glory. It's about ensuring that when the credits roll on your personal movie, it ends exactly the way you want it to.

So, are you ready to become the director of your final scene? To craft a send-off so perfect your great-grandkids will be talking about it decades from now?

Because that's what funeral planning really is. It's not just important - it's essential. It's your last chance to say "I love you", "I'm sorry", "Thank you", and "Remember me" all at once.

It's your final act of kindness, your last hurrah, your ultimate swan-song.

And trust me, it's going to be legendary.

A question for you. Which family members should I share this with?

The Emotional and Practical Benefits of Planning.

Imagine gifting your loved ones a map when they're lost in the darkest moment of their lives. Because that's how planning your funeral will look like – a beacon of light in the storm of grief.

Let's cut to the chase: Death is a sucker punch to the gut, leaving families reeling. But preplanning? It's like emotional armor, softening the blow when it matters most.

Think about it. Your family's just lost you – their rock, their compass, their go-to for dad jokes. They're shattered, barely able to decide what to have for dinner, let alone make a hundred decisions about your final send-off. But you, you magnificent planner you, have already taken care of it all.

The result? Instead of drowning in a sea of choices, they're floating on the raft you built. They're not arguing over whether you'd want "My Way" or "Highway to Hell" – they're sharing stories, laughing through tears, and honoring you exactly as you wished.

But the benefits of pre planning aren't just emotional – they're practical as well.

First up: Money talks. Funerals can cost a pretty penny, often hitting families when they're financially vulnerable. Preplanning lets you lock in today's prices, potentially saving you thousands of dollars. It's like letting your wallet time-travel to outsmart inflation.

Then there's the stress factor. Preplanning is like hiring a personal assistant to handle the administration and logistical hurdles in your afterlife. No more frantic searches for important documents or last-minute scrambles for funeral funds. You've handled it, like the boss you are.

But here's where it gets really good: preplanning gives you the power to write your own ending. Want a Viking-themed funeral? A space burial? A biodegradable tree pod? Whatever floats your boat (or burns it, in the case of a Viking send-off), you can make it happen. It's your story — end it your way.

Then, let's talk about the elephant in the room - family dynamics. We all have that uncle who thinks he knows best, or those siblings who bicker over everything. Preplanning silences the squabbles before they start. Your wishes are clear, concise, and, most importantly, yours.

But perhaps the most profound benefit is the gift of presence. When you've preplanned, your loved ones can focus on the things that matter — remembering you, supporting each other, and healing. They're not bogged down by logistics; they're free to feel, to grieve, to celebrate your life.

Preplanning isn't just smart - it's an act of love. It's telling your family, "I've got this, even when I'm gone." It's ensuring that your last impact on this earth is one of kindness, foresight, and care.

So, what's the bottom line? Preplanning isn't about dwelling on death - it's about embracing life. It's about taking control, leaving a legacy, and giving your loved ones the space to remember you with joy rather than stress.

It's your final gift, your last hurrah, your ultimate "I love you."

And trust me, it's the best present you'll ever give — one they'll thank you for long after you're gone.

Addressing Common Misconceptions about Funerals

Funerals: The land of black veils, somber faces, and enough flowers to make a botanist swoon. But hold on to your hat, because we're about to shatter some funeral myths faster than you can say "ashes to ashes."

Myth #1: Funerals are always gloomy affairs.

Reality check: Who says you can't go out with a bang? Modern funerals can be as vibrant as a Mardi Gras parade. From confetti cannons to rock concerts, the only limit is your imagination. But it's okay for it to be simple too. Remember, it's a celebration of life, not a competition for who can look the most miserable.

Myth #2: You need a fancy casket to show you care.

Newsflash: Love isn't measured in mahogany and gold plating. That overpriced box? It's going six feet under, never to be seen again. Instead of splurging on a casket, why not use the money to invest in experiences your loved ones can cherish? A scholarship fund or a donation to a favorite cause says a lot more than a shiny coffin.

Myth #3: Embalming is always necessary.

Hold your horses, chemical lovers. Unless you're planning a cross-country tour with the deceased, embalming is often optional. Natural burials are gaining popularity faster than you can say "eco-friendly." Your body can return to the earth almost as naturally as it came, no formaldehyde required.

Myth #4: Funeral homes are your only option.

Wrong-O! Home funerals are experiencing a revival, much like vinyl records. With the right guidance, you can host a heartfelt send-off in your living room, backyard, or even at a beloved beach. It's personal, intimate, and more affordable than traditional options.

Myth #5: Cremation is the cheapest option.

Not so fast, penny-pinchers. While cremation can be cost-effective, it's not always the budget winner. Direct burials or donating your body to science can sometimes be even more wallet-friendly. Plus, have you seen the price of some of those fancy urns? You could buy a small car for that amount!

Myth #6: Children should be shielded from funerals.

Oh, please. Kids are tougher than we give them credit for. Excluding them from the funeral process can lead to confusion and unresolved grief. With proper explanation and support, funerals can help children understand and cope with loss. Plus, they often bring a refreshing honesty to the proceedings. Out of the mouths of babes, right?

Myth #7: You need a religious service.

Holy moly, that's not true! Non-religious or humanist funerals are on the rise faster than a hallelujah chorus. Your send-off can be as secular as a science textbook or as spiritual as a moonlight meditation. The key is authenticity – make it true to who you were.

Myth #8: Funerals are for the dead.

Plot twist: Funerals are for the living. They present a chance for the grieving to come together, share memories, and begin the healing process. When planning, think about what will bring comfort and meaning to those left behind.

Myth #9: Once the funeral's over, the grieving should too.

Oh honey, if only it were that simple. Grief doesn't punch a timecard. It's a journey, not a sprint. The funeral is just the beginning of the healing process, not the finish line.

Myth #10: Funeral planning is morbid.

Wrong again! It's actually an act of love. By planning ahead, you're saving your family from stress, potential conflicts, and financial burden during an already difficult time. It's like leaving them a roadmap when they're lost in the woods of grief.

Now, funeral myths have been busted wide open. Remember, your farewell should be as unique as your fingerprint. Don't let outdated ideas box you in. After all, it's your party, and you'll celebrate your life how you want to!

Key Takeaways: Mastering Your Final Act

- Death's timing is unpredictable, but your response doesn't have to be.
- Preplanning saves more than money – it saves sanity and disagreements.
- Your funeral, your rules – make it as unique as your fingerprint.
- It's not about the price of the casket – it's about the value of your legacy.

Bottom line: Planning your farewell isn't about death – it's about life. Your life. In all its messy, beautiful and unique glory.

Now it's your turn:

What's the one thing or qualities you want people to remember about you when you're gone?

_____

_____

_____

_____

Next up: We're diving into the emotional rollercoaster of grief. Fasten your seatbelts - it's going to be a meaningful ride.

CHAPTER 2:

Navigating the Emotional Journey - Coping with Grief and Loss

From planning your grand finale, we now turn to the raw, beating heart of loss. Grief — it's the uninvited guest that crashes your life's party, overstays its welcome, and rearranges your emotional furniture without permission.

You've scripted your perfect exit, but for those left behind, the real performance is just beginning. Welcome to the most intense, unpredictable rollercoaster ride you never bought a ticket for.

Grief doesn't play by the rules. It's not a neatly packaged five-stage process you can check off like a to-do list. It's more like a Jackson Pollock painting — chaotic, messy and deeply personal. One day you're laughing at a fond memory, the next you're sobbing into your cereal because they're not there to burn the toast.

Here's the truth bomb: There's no "right" way to grieve. Your journey through loss is as unique as your fingerprint. Some people wail while some go silent. Some throw themselves into work while others can barely get out of bed. And guess what? It's all okay.

But while grief is a solo expedition, you don't have to navigate it alone. Think of support systems as your emotional GPS. From friends, family, support groups to therapists - these are all coordinates on your map towards healing. Use them. Lean on them. Let them be your compass to guide you in this journey.

Grief isn't just a mental experience – it's a physical one too. Your body might betray you in ways you never expected. Insomnia, loss of appetite, aches in places you didn't know could ache. It's not just in your head – it's in your cells, your bones, your very DNA. So, be kind to your body. Nourish it, rest it, move it. Your physical self is grieving too.

Now, let's talk about the grief police – those well-meaning folks who think they know exactly how you should be feeling. "It's been a month, shouldn't you be over it by now?" or "At least they lived a long life." Newsflash: There's no expiration date on grief, and making comparisons over how one grieves are about as useful as a chocolate teapot. Your grief, your rules.

But here's where it gets interesting. Grief, believe it or not, can be transformative. It's the ultimate reality check, stripping away the trivial and leaving you raw, real, and often with a new perspective on life. Many people report feeling more compassionate, more appreciative of small joys and more connected to others after loss. It's not a silver lining - it's more like a hard-won battle scar that changes you forever.

So, how do you cope? You breathe. You feel. You honor your loss. Create rituals that speak to your soul - whether it's lighting a candle, visiting a special place, or belting out their favorite song at the top of your lungs. Find ways to keep their memory alive that feel authentic to you.

And remember, healing isn't about "getting over" the loss. It's about learning to carry it with you, integrating it into your life's story. The pain may soften, but the love remains. That's the paradox of grief - it's the price we pay for the privilege of having loved deeply.

As you navigate this emotional odyssey, remember the wisdom of your preplanning. In those moments when grief fogs your mind, you'll have a clear path forward, free from the added stress of funeral decisions. It's your final gift to your loved ones – a beacon in their darkest hour.

Grief is the final frontier of love. It's messy, it's painful, but it's also a testament to the depth of your connections with others. So feel it, honor it, let it transform you. After all, that's what life and death are all about.

Your turn.

What's the one thing you want them to remember in their grief?

_____

For me, I had a bloody great life and lived every day to the max, so don't be sad!

The Role of Rituals in the Healing Process

From the chaotic canvas of grief, we now turn to the brushstrokes that bring order to the chaos – rituals. These aren't just empty gestures or outdated traditions; they're the anchors that will keep us steady in the storm of loss.

Rituals are the bridge between the world we knew and the one we're forced to navigate without our loved ones. They're the GPS for our hearts when our emotional compasses are spinning wildly.

Think of rituals as the punctuation marks in the run-on sentence of grief. They give us pause, structure, and meaning when everything else feels senseless. Whether it's lighting a candle on their birthdays, wearing their favorite sweater, or continuing their annual holiday traditions, these acts connect us to our loved ones in tangible ways.

But here's the magic – rituals aren't one-size-fits-all. They're as unique as the relationship you shared with them. Maybe it's planting a tree in their memory, creating a scholarship in their name or simply making their famous lasagna recipe. The power lies not in the act itself but in the intention and meaning you pour into it.

Rituals serve multiple purposes in the healing process. They provide:

1. Continuity: A thread that connects your past with your present and future.
2. Control: In a situation where you feel powerless, rituals provide a sense of control and agency. They offer structure and a way to take meaningful action, helping you regain a feeling of ownership over the situation, even when things seem beyond your control.
3. Comfort: A familiar action in unfamiliar emotional territory.
4. Community: Shared rituals bring people together, reminding us we're not alone in our grief.
5. Catharsis: A safe space to express emotions that might otherwise stay bottled up.

The beauty of rituals is that they evolve with us. What brought comfort in the raw and early days of grief may change as time passes. That's okay. Your rituals can grow and shift as you do.

Did you remember the preplanning you did for your own farewell? Those choices you made are rituals too – ones that will guide and comfort your loved ones when you're gone. Your favorite song, that quirky dress code, the donation in lieu of flowers - these are the gifts you're leaving behind, the stepping stones for their healing journey.

But don't wait for loss to embrace the power of rituals. Start now. Create traditions with your loved ones that celebrate your connections with them. These become the threads that will weave comfort into the fabric of grief when the time comes.

Rituals also help us redefine our relationship with the person we've lost. They transform our loved ones from a painful absence into a cherished presence. Through rituals, we learn that love doesn't end with death –

it simply changes form.

Some might dismiss rituals as superstitious or unnecessary. But science backs up their power. Studies show that rituals can reduce anxiety, increase feelings of control and even alleviate grief. They're not magic spells, but they are magical in their ability to heal.

As you navigate the choppy waters of grief, let rituals be your life raft. They won't make the pain disappear, but they'll give you a moment of respite or a breath of fresh air when you feel like you're drowning in sorrow. There's no "right" way to do rituals. The only rule is that it must mean something to you. So light that candle, visit that special place, tell that inside joke. In doing so, you're not just honoring your loved one — you're honoring your own journey through grief.

Rituals are the love letters we write to those we've lost and to ourselves. They're the compasses that guide us through the wilderness of grief, back to a place where joy and sorrow can coexist. So embrace them, create them and let them heal you. After all, isn't that what this journey is all about?

Communicating with Family Members about Funeral Arrangements

From the personal solace of rituals, we now zoom out to the wider circle of family dynamics. Talking about funeral arrangements with your loved ones isn't just a conversation - it's an art form, a delicate dance between honesty and sensitivity.

Picture this: You've done the hard work. You've planned your grand exit, chosen between a disco inferno cremation or a tree-hugging green burial. But your masterpiece is still a secret, locked away like the last season of your favorite Netflix show. What good is a plan if no one knows about it?

Enter the family pow-wow. It's time to spill the beans about this book, your wishes, and why you've decided to take death by the horns.

First things first: Who needs to be in on this secret? Start with your inner circle - your spouse, kids, siblings. These are your front-row guests, the ones who'll be carrying out your final wishes. But don't stop there. Consider the supporting cast - close friends, your legal eagle (aka lawyer), and perhaps that cousin who always knows how to lighten the mood.

Now, for the million-dollar question: How do you drop this bomb without causing a family meltdown?

Timing is everything. Don't spring this on Aunt Martha during Thanksgiving dinner or tell your kids right before their big job interview. Choose a moment when everyone's relaxed, preferably not in the middle of a family feud about who makes the best potato salad.

Set the stage. This isn't a casual "Hey, I decided to dye my hair purple" conversation. Give them a heads up. "I've been doing some important planning, and I'd like to share it with you." It sets the tone without sending everyone into a panic.

Be prepared for a rollercoaster of reactions. Some might be relieved, others might get emotional, and a few might look at you like you've grown a second head. That's okay. Everyone processes differently. Your job isn't to control their reactions, but to communicate clearly and lovingly.

Here's a pro tip: Frame it as an act of love. Because that's exactly what it is. You're not being morbid; you're being mighty thoughtful. You're lifting a burden off their shoulders during what will be an incredibly tough time.

Now, about this book. Treat it like your favorite recipe - one that's meant to be shared, not hidden away in a dusty drawer. Let them know it exists, where to find it, and why you've created it. It's your roadmap for them, a gift of clarity in the fog of grief.

But remember, this isn't a monologue. It's a dialogue. Listen to their thoughts, answer their questions, be open to their input. You might be surprised by their insights or learn something new about their wishes too.

And here's the kicker - this conversation isn't one and done. It's an ongoing dialogue. As your wishes evolve or circumstances change, keep them in the loop. It's like updating your social media status, but way more important.

Lastly, don't forget the power of humor. Yes, we're talking about your eventual departure from this mortal coil, but that doesn't mean it has to be all doom and gloom. Share a laugh about that ridiculous song you want played or the crazy outfit you've chosen. Laughter can be the spoonful of sugar that helps this medicine go down.

Keep in mind, by having this conversation, you're not just communicating about funeral arrangements. You're opening up a space for your family to talk about life, death, and everything in between. It's an opportunity for connection, understanding and love.

So go ahead, break the ice. Share your plans. Let them in on the secret. After all, your farewell party is going to be legendary - it'd be a shame not to give them a sneak preview.

Who will be in charge of your plans?

_____

Who Should Arrange What and What Part?

Now that you've dropped the funeral planning bombshell on your loved ones, it's time to delegate. Think of it as casting roles for your final production - everyone has a part to play, and you're the director calling the shots from beyond.

Assigning tasks isn't just about efficiency; it's about involvement. It gives your loved ones a sense of purpose, a way to channel their grief into action. Plus, it prevents that one control-freak cousin from taking over the whole show (we all have one, admit it).

First up: The Ringleader. This is your right-hand person, the one who'll orchestrate your grand finale. Choose someone who's organized, level-headed, and can handle pressure like a pro. They'll be the go-to for all things funeral, the captain of your farewell ship.

Next, consider your Creative Director. Got a friend with an eye for design? Let them handle the visuals - from the funeral program to the photo displays. They'll make sure your aesthetic game is strong, even when you're not there to approve the font choices.

Don't forget the Master of Ceremonies. This is the person who'll lead the service, share stories, and keep things flowing. Pick someone who can strike the right balance between poignant and humorous, someone who really gets you.

Now, for the nitty-gritty:

- The Paperwork Guru: Legal documents, death certificates, insurance claims - not glamorous, but crucial. Assign this to your most detail-oriented family member.
- The Guestlist Guru: Someone needs to spread the word and handle RSVPs. Your social butterfly friend? Perfect for the job.
- The Melody Maker: Music sets the tone. Let your audiophile buddy curate the playlist that'll have people tapping their toes even as they dab their eyes.
- The Flower Child: Floral arrangements, eco-friendly alternatives, or that weird succulent collection you requested - put your green-thumbed pal in charge.

- The Food Fairy: Because let's face it, food is comfort. Your culinary wizard friend can handle the catering or potluck coordination.
- The Tech Whiz: Live Streaming for far-flung friends, a photo slideshow, or that hologram of you doing the Macarena - your tech-savvy niece can make it happen.
- The Comfort Crew: Assign a few empathetic souls to be on emotional support duty, armed with tissues and hugs.

This isn't about burdening people; it's about giving them a chance to contribute, to feel useful in a time when many feel helpless. It's therapeutic, turning grief into action.

But here's the plot twist - while you're assigning roles, leave room for spontaneity. Some of the most meaningful contributions might come from unexpected places. Maybe your shy nephew writes a beautiful eulogy, or your clumsy brother-in-law arranges the most stunning floral display.

And don't forget to assign someone the role of 'Keeper of the Perspective.' This person's job? To remind everyone that amidst the planning and the stress, the goal is to celebrate your life, not to achieve funeral perfection.

Now, consider leaving a wild card task - something unexpected that aligns with your personality. A flash mob at the cemetery? A scavenger hunt for your hidden messages? Let your creativity run wild.

By divvying up the responsibilities, you're not just planning a funeral; you're creating collaborative artwork. Each person adds their own touch and color to the canvas of your farewell.

So, go ahead, hand out those roles like you're casting for an Oscar-winning movie. Because in the end, this isn't just about planning your exit - it's about bringing your loved ones together, one last time, in a celebration that's uniquely and undeniably you.

Key Takeaways:

- Grief is as unique as a fingerprint - there's no "right" way to mourn.
- Your support system is your emotional GPS - use it shamelessly.
- Grief isn't just a mental experience - it's a physical one too. Be kind to your body.
- There's no expiration date on grief. Ignore the "grief police."
- Rituals are powerful tools for healing - create ones that resonate with you.
- Communicating about funeral plans is an act of love, not morbidity.
- Delegate funeral tasks - it gives loved ones purpose and prevents power struggles.
- Sharing your wishes isn't just planning; it's your final gift to your family.

The Final Scene: *Your pre planning isn't just about you - it's a lifeline for those left behind.*

Your Director's Cut: *What ritual or memory-keeping practice would bring you comfort?*

_____

_____

_____

CHAPTER 3:

Legal and Financial Considerations

Understanding Legal Requirements for Funerals

From casting your farewell's starring roles, we pivot to the backstage legalities - the fine print of your final curtain call. Strap in, because we're about to make legal jargon sexy (or at least less snooze-inducing).

Think of funeral laws as the guardrails on your highway to the great beyond. They're not there to cramp your style but to ensure your grand exit is as smooth as your favorite whiskey.

First up: The Death Certificate - your post-life passport. Without it, you're stuck in bureaucratic limbo. It's not just a piece of paper; it's the key that unlocks everything from closing bank accounts to transferring assets. Pro tip: Order multiple copies. Your loved ones will thank you when they're not playing document tag with every institution under the sun.

Next, let's talk about body logistics. Sounds morbid? Maybe. Necessary? Absolutely. Each state has its own rules about how long you can chill (literally) before the funeral. Some places insist on embalming if you're not taking the express route to your final resting place. Others are cool with refrigeration. Know the rules, or risk turning your funeral into a game of beat-the-clock.

Burial laws are another beast. Want to be buried in your backyard next to Fluffy? Not so fast. Zoning laws have opinions about where you can plant your permanent garden. And if you're going for a green burial, make sure it's legal in your area. Mother Nature may love you, but local ordinances may not.

Cremation more your style? There's paperwork for that too. You'll need a cremation authorization form, typically signed by your next of kin. And no, you can't just scatter ashes wherever the wind takes you. Some places require permits while others ban it entirely. Don't let your final wish land your loved ones in legal hot water.

Now, for the plot twist: Funeral homes aren't legally required for everything. You can have a home funeral in most states, but there are rules. It's like throwing a party but with more paperwork and fewer balloon animals.

Speaking of funeral homes - they're required to give you an itemized price list. It's not just good manners; it's the law. The Funeral Rule is your consumer protection superhero, ensuring you're not upsold on a gold-plated casket when you want a simple pine box.

Let's not forget the will - your posthumous playlist. Without it, the state decides who gets your vintage record collection and that embarrassing diary from high school. A clear, legally sound will is like leaving a detailed map instead of a vague "X marks the spot."

But wait, there's more! Power of Attorney and Advanced Directives are your dynamic duo for end-of-life decisions. They ensure your wishes are respected when you can't speak for yourself. Think of them as your legal body doubles, stepping in when you're not able to call the shots.

Here's a curveball: Organ donation laws. If you're planning to donate, make sure your wishes are crystal clear and legally documented. It's your chance to be a superhero after the credits roll on your life story.

Navigating these laws might seem like trying to solve a Rubik's Cube blindfolded, but here's the silver lining: Understanding them now means less stress for your loved ones later. It's like leaving them a cheat sheet for the toughest exam they'll ever face.

Laws vary by state faster than fashion trends. What's kosher in California might be a no-go in New York. Do your homework, or better yet, consult a legal eagle who specializes in end-of-life planning.

By mastering these legal considerations, you're not just planning a funeral; you're crafting a legality-proof legacy. It's your final act of love, ensuring your exit is as flawless as your entrance into this world (minus the crying and diapers, hopefully).

Creating a Budget for Funeral Expenses

From the labyrinth of legal requirements, we now turn to the dollars and cents of your grand finale. Money talks, even when you're not around to chat anymore. So, let's crunch some numbers and make your funeral budget sing.

Picture this: Your loved ones, already grappling with grief, are suddenly faced with a financial Everest. Not exactly the parting gift you had in mind, right? That's where your fiscal foresight comes in, turning a potential money pit into a manageable molehill.

First things first: Funerals aren't cheap. They're like weddings, but with less champagne and more tissues. The average funeral can set you back anywhere from $7,000 to $12,000. That's a chunk of change that could buy a used car or fund a killer vacation. But fear not, budget maestro - with some clever planning, you can orchestrate a send-off that's both meaningful and economical.

Let's break it down, shall we?

1. The Main Event: The funeral service itself. This includes the venue, officiant and basic décor. Pro tip: Consider alternative venues. Your favorite park or beloved

community center could slash costs while amping up the personal touch.

2. The After-Party: Reception costs. Food, drinks, and a space for people to gather and reminisce. Potlucks aren't just for church basements anymore. They can be a heartwarming way to involve everyone.

3. The Paperwork Parade: Death certificates, permits, and other bureaucratic necessities. These nickel-and-dime expenses add up faster than you can say "red tape."

4. The Final Ride: Transportation for you (yes, you need a lift) and possibly for the funeral attendees.

5. The Eternal Real Estate: Cemetery plot or cremation costs. Cremation is generally cheaper, but if you're set on a burial, consider sharing a plot. Cozy, isn't it?

6. The Coffin Conundrum: Your final resting place. Remember, you can't take it with you, so maybe skip the mahogany with gold inlay.

7. The Glam Squad: Body preparation, including embalming if that's your jam. Going au naturel can save a pretty penny.

8. The Announcement: Obituary and funeral program printing. Digital options can cut costs and trees simultaneously.

9. The Flower Power: Floral arrangements. Consider in-season blooms or meaningful alternatives like favorite books or photos.

10. The Extras: Things like memorial videos, guest books, or that life-sized ice sculpture of you doing the Macarena.

Now, here's where it gets interesting. You've got options, my friend. Want to prepay and lock in today's prices? Go for it. Prefer to set up a payable-upon-death account? That works too. Just stashing cash under your mattress? Well, at least make sure someone knows it's there.

The goal isn't to see how little you can spend. It's about creating a meaningful experience without leaving your loved ones in financial turmoil. Think of it as your last investment in their peace of mind.

Here's a radical thought: Talk to your family about this budget. I know, discussing money feels about as comfortable as a corset made of cacti. But it's crucial. You might discover that what you think is important doesn't align with their wishes. Maybe they'd rather skip the fancy casket and use that money for a scholarship in your name.

Lastly, don't forget to factor in inflation. Today's $10,000 funeral might be tomorrow's $15,000 send-off. Building in a buffer is like leaving a generous tip for the cosmic waiter.

By creating this budget, you're not just planning a funeral. You're crafting a financial roadmap, a final act of love that says, "I've got this handled. You focus on remembering the good times." Now that's what I call going out in style - fiscally responsible style, that is.

Exploring Options for Prepaying or Prearranging Funeral Services

Now that we've crunched the numbers, let's talk about footing the bill for your final shindig before you've even RSVP'd to the afterlife. Prepaying for your funeral isn't just forward-thinking; it's like leaving a financial care package for your loved ones.

Picture this: You're gone, and your family is free to focus on sharing stories and ugly-crying into the fancy tissues, instead of playing "How are we going to pay for this?" Bingo! That's the magic of preplanning and prepaying.

Let's break down your options, shall we?

1.   Funeral Insurance: It's like life insurance's quirky cousin. You pay premiums, and when you kick the bucket, it covers your funeral costs. Simple, right? But watch out for the fine print - some policies have more strings attached than a marionette convention.

2. Prepaid Funeral Plans: This is where you waltz into a funeral home, plan your send-off, and pay for it upfront. It's like buying a ticket for a concert that you'll never attend (but everyone else will enjoy). Pros: You lock in today's prices. Cons: If the funeral home goes belly-up, your money might vanish faster than a magician's rabbit.

3. Totten Trust (aka Payable on Death Account): This is your financial superhero. Set up a bank account, name a beneficiary, and voila! When you die, they get immediate access to the funds without the hassle of probate. It's like a fiscal fast-pass to your funeral funds.

4. Pre-need Trust: Similar to a prepaid plan, but with more legal protections. Your money goes into a trust, often managed by a third party. It's like putting your funeral funds in a financial fortress.

5. Savings Account: Old school, but effective. Open a separate high-yield savings account earmarked for your funeral. It's not fancy, but it gets the job done.

Now, here's where it gets juicy: Setting up a separate account now. This isn't just smart; it's genius with a cherry on top. Why? Let me count the ways:

1. Peace of Mind: You know the money's there, growing like a well-fertilized plant.

2. Easy Access: Your family won't have to go on a financial scavenger hunt.

3. Interest Accrual: Your funeral fund can earn its own allowance while you're still kicking.

4. Flexibility: Change your mind about that Viking funeral? No problem. The money's yours to reallocate.

5. Tax Benefits: In some cases, these accounts can offer tax advantages. Consult your friendly neighborhood tax guru for details.

When setting up this account, consider these pro tips:

- Name a trusted beneficiary. Choose wisely - this person will be the Frodo to your funeral fund ring.
- Keep the account details with your other important documents. Don't make your family play "Where's Waldo?" with your finances.
- Regularly review and adjust the amount. Inflation waits for no one, not even the dead.
- Consider splitting your funds between a prepaid plan and a separate account for maximum flexibility.

Prepaying for your funeral isn't about being morbid. It's about being mighty considerate. It's your final "I love you, I've got this" to your family. You're essentially throwing them a financial life preserver in a sea of grief.

By exploring these options and setting up a separate account now, you're not just planning a funeral. You're orchestrating a symphony of financial foresight. You're ensuring that when the curtain falls on your life's performance, the only drama will be in the eulogies, not in the bill-paying. Be the Mozart of funeral finances. Compose a masterpiece of fiscal responsibility that'll have your loved ones applauding your prudence long after you've taken your final bow.

Key Takeaways:

- Death certificates are your posthumous passport - order multiple copies.
- Know your state's laws on body preservation and burial - they're as varied as pizza toppings.
- Your will is your posthumous playlist - make it clear and legally sound.
- Funeral costs can rival a small wedding - budget wisely.
- Prepaying for your funeral is like leaving a financial care package for your loved ones.
- Consider setting up a separate funeral savings account - it's your fiscal fast-pass.

- Explore all payment options - from funeral insurance to Totten Trusts.
- The Funeral Rule is your consumer protection superhero - know your rights.
- Power of Attorney and Advanced Directives are your dynamic duo for end-of-life decisions.
- Regular reviewing of your plans is crucial - death waits for no one, but laws and prices change.

The Bottom Line: *Financial foresight isn't morbid, it's mighty considerate.*

Your Fiscal Reflection: *What's your biggest concern about funeral costs, and how can you address it now?*

_____

_____

_____

CHAPTER 4:

Types of Funeral Services – Traditional Burials vs. Cremation

From fiscal foresight to final farewells, we're now stepping into the ring for the ultimate showdown: Traditional Burials vs. Cremation. It's the heavyweight championship of the afterlife, folks!

In one corner, we have the classic contender: Traditional Burials. It's been around since the dawn of civilization, the comfort food of funeral options. Picture it: You, snug as a bug in a rug, nestled six feet under in your own little patch of forever real estate. It's the choice for those who want to leave a lasting mark – quite literally – on the earth.

A traditional burial is like the vinyl record of death – old school, tangible, and with a certain nostalgic charm. It gives your loved ones a physical place to visit, to lay flowers and to have heart-to-heart conversations with your headstone. It's permanent and unchanging – a rock-solid reminder of your existence in an ever-changing world.

But let's not sugarcoat it - a traditional burial comes with baggage. It's the most expensive option, often costing as much as a small car. And let's talk real estate. Cemetery plots are the beachfront property of the death industry - prime and pricey. Plus, there's the environmental impact to consider. Embalming fluids and non-biodegradable caskets aren't exactly Mother Nature's best friends.

Now, in the other corner, we have the modern maverick: Cremation. Think of it as the Marie Kondo of funeral options - minimalist, efficient, and growing in popularity. Essentially, you're being transformed into ashes, neatly contained in something about the size of a large coffee can. Okay, maybe that's a bit blunt, but you get the idea!

Cremation is like the Swiss Army knife of the funeral world - versatile and practical. Want your ashes scattered in your favorite fishing spot? Done. Fancy being turned into a diamond or shot into space? Cremation has got you covered. It's the choice for the adventurous soul, the traveler, the one who says, "Why be tied down in death when I wasn't in life?"

Cost-wise, cremation is often cheaper than a traditional burial, leaving more in the kitty for that epic wake you've always dreamed of. It's also more environmentally friendly, assuming you're not having your ashes scattered from a gas-guzzling airplane.

But cremation isn't all roses and rainbows. Some find the idea of being reduced to ashes a bit too... final. There's no going back and no changing your mind. For some cultures and religions, cremation is a big no-no.

So, how do you choose? Here's the plot twist - it's not just about you. Your decision will impact how your loved ones grieve and remember you. A traditional burial might offer them a place of pilgrimage, a physical connection to your memory. Cremation could give them the freedom to honor you in unique and personal ways.

Consider your values. Are you all about tradition or do you march to the beat of your own drum? Is the impact to the environment a big concern? How about cost? And let's not forget personal preferences — some people are simply creeped out by the idea of worms having a field day with their remains.

Remember, there's no right or wrong choice here. It's about what feels right for you and your loved ones. Whether you choose to be planted like a seed or go up in a blaze of glory, what matters most is the life you lived, not how your physical form is handled after you've left the building.

In the end, whether you're Team Burial or Team Cremation, you're making a choice that reflects who you are and how you want to be remembered. It's your final statement, your last hurrah, your ultimate mic drop. So choose wisely, choose personally, and maybe leave a little room for humor. After all, who says you can't have the last laugh?

Alternative Funeral Options (Green Burials, Home Funerals, etc.)

If a traditional burial or cremation feels too mainstream for your final bow, fear not! The funeral industry has more plot twists than a soap opera, offering alternative options that'll make your exit as unique as your Instagram feed.

First up: Green Burials. It's like composting, but for humans. You're returning to nature faster than a hippie at Woodstock. No embalming fluids, no concrete vaults, just you and Mother Earth in a biodegradable embrace. Imagine being wrapped in a shroud or placed in a wicker casket, becoming one with the soil. It's the circle of life, Mufasa-style. Green burials are for the eco-warriors, the tree-huggers, and anyone who wants their last act to be a love letter to the planet.

But why stop there? How about becoming a tree? With bio-urns, your ashes can nourish a sapling. It's like reincarnation but with better roots. Imagine your great-grandkids having a picnic under your branches. Talk about family trees!

Now, for the homebodies: Home Funerals. It's exactly what it sounds like - keeping things in-house, literally. Your living room becomes a funeral center. It's intimate, personal and budget-friendly. Plus, it gives a whole new meaning to "home is where the heart is." Home funerals are for those who want to keep it real, raw, and close to the family hearth.

For the aquatically inclined, there's the Sea Burial. It's like a Viking funeral, minus the flaming arrows. Your ashes are placed in a biodegradable urn and released into the ocean. Perfect for mermaids-at-heart or those who always wanted to sleep with the fishes (in a non-mobster way).

Feeling a bit more... explosive? Consider having your ashes turned into fireworks. Go out with a bang, painting the sky in a blaze of glory. It's apyrotechnic's dream and guaranteed to be a finale no one will forget.

For the scholarly types, body donation is like the ultimate group project. You're contributing to medical research, helping train future doctors, or advancing forensic science. It's education beyond the grave — you'll be the coolest teacher ever.

Space burial is for the stargazers and sci-fi enthusiasts. A portion of your ashes can hitch a ride on a rocket and orbit Earth or even land on the Moon. It's one small step for man, one giant leap for your remains.

Diamondification (yes, it's a thing) turns your ashes into a real diamond. It's pressure and heat, baby — just like how you lived your life. Wear-your-loved-one jewelry brings a whole new meaning to "family jewels".

Mummification isn't just for ancient Egyptians anymore. Modern mummification services offer a way to preserve yourself for posterity. It's for those who really, really want to stick around.

And for the artists, how about having your ashes mixed into paint for a portrait? You'll literally be the Mona Lisa of your family — a conversation starter for generations to come.

These alternative options aren't just about being quirky; they're about aligning your final act with your values, personality and legacy. They offer a way to make your farewell as unique as your fingerprint, as memorable as your best joke, and as impactful as your loudest laugh.

Your funeral is your last performance, your final statement. Whether you choose to feed a tree, light up the sky, or orbit the Earth, make it quintessentially you. After all, why be ordinary in death when you were extraordinary in life? Think outside the pine box. Your farewell can be as creative, eco-friendly, or out-of-this-world as you are. It's not just about how you lived; it's about how you want to be remembered. Make it count, make it you, and maybe, just maybe, make them smile even as they say goodbye.

Customizing The Funeral Service to Reflect the Life of the Deceased

From green burials to space odysseys, we've explored the wild frontier of funeral options. But now, let's zoom in on the main event: your funeral service. This isn't just any performance - it's your lifetime achievement award ceremony, your personal Oscars, your magnum opus.

Customizing your funeral is like curating the ultimate playlist of your life. It's about turning a somber occasion into a standing ovation for your unique journey. Think less "Ding Dong, the Witch is Dead" and more "My Way" (unless, of course, you were actually a witch, in which case, rock that theme).

Start with the venue. Who says it has to be a church or funeral home? If you spent more time on the golf course than in a pew, why not have your service on the 18th hole? Beach bum? Let the waves be your backdrop. Bookworm? The local library could be your final chapter setting.

Now, let's talk about the atmosphere. Ditch the organ dirges for a soundtrack that screams "you". Were you a rock 'n' roll rebel? Crank up the AC/DC. Opera aficionado? Let Pavarotti serenade your departure. Create a playlist that makes people say, "Yep, that's definitely them."

Visuals matter too. Instead of formal portraits, plaster the place with candid shots - you ugly-laughing, you covered in birthday cake, you in that ridiculous Halloween costume. Let your personality shine through every image.

Forget stuffy eulogies. Encourage storytelling. Let your best friend recount that hilarious road trip fiasco. Have your grandkids share the terrible dad jokes you always told. It's about painting a vibrant picture of your life, warts and all.

Dress code? Make it reflect you. If you lived in band t-shirts and jeans, why should your guests suffer in black suits? Hawaiian shirts, superhero costumes, or pajamas – whatever fits your vibe.

Consider interactive elements. Did you love puzzles? Leave a crossword about your life for guests to solve. Karaoke fan? Set up a booth for brave souls to belt out your favorite tunes.

Food and drinks should scream "you" too. Your famous chili recipe, your addiction to gummy bears, that weird pizza topping combination you swore by – let your quirks shine through the menu.

Don't forget take-homes. Instead of prayer cards, how about seed packets of your favorite flowers? Or mini bottles of your signature cocktail? Give them something to remember you by that's actually... memorable.

If you were a prankster, plan one last laugh. A surprise video message from you, a confetti cannon during a solemn moment, or a flash mob – keep them guessing till the end.

For the grand finale, think big. A sky lantern release, a group dance to your favorite song, or a collective toast with your preferred poison. Go out with a bang, not a whimper.

This is your show. It's okay to be unconventional, to break the mold, to make people smile through their tears. Your funeral should be a reflection of your life – colorful, unique, and true to who you were.

By customizing your service, you're not just planning a funeral. You're crafting a celebration, a tribute, a final bow that's as unique as your fingerprint. It's your last chance to remind everyone of who you were, what you loved, and how you lived. Plan a send-off that's so perfect for you, it'll have people saying, "Well, they certainly went out in style." After all, if you can't have it your way at your own funeral, when can you?

Wishes and Whispers: Our Final Requests

Before we roll the credits on this chapter, let's take a moment to get personal. After all, this isn't just theory - it's about real people making real choices. So, let me share a little about my own wishes, and those of my husband:

Jenni's Wish: When my time comes, I want to be cremated before the service. No urn for me, just a bright blue box, the same color as my eyes. I'd like it to sit surrounded by my collection of colorful Skechers. The ceremony? I want it at home, with my niece leading the way. As it starts, I want everyone holding a glass of Pimms, with "Thank You for Being a Friend" by Andrew Gold playing in the background.

The food should be simple but full of my favorites – pork bites, prawns, salmon, and, of course, mini donuts with mock cream and shortbread. When it's time to share memories, I'd love Rex B to talk about my adventurous twenties overseas, while Abe A joins via livestream from the UK, reminiscing about my recruitment days. Leigh O should speak of our friendship, and Louise A can bring up all the fun we've had over the decades. Richard K and Mel S will tell stories of the motorhome days – those were special times.

As for my ashes, they'll be reunited with my mother and father. There's something deeply comforting about being together, even in our final rest.

Duncan's Wish: Duncan, ever the romantic adventurer, has his own

unique plans. He wants to be cremated, but only after the funeral service. His ashes will take one final journey—half will rest with his beloved first wife, Jenny No. 1, while the other half will be scattered on the lake where we spent every summer boating. It's as if he's splitting his eternity between his two great loves.

For the service, he wants a coffin adorned with one of his cherished yachts, held at his local church, followed by drinks at his favorite workingmen's club. True to his spirit, Duncan wants to leave behind a recorded message in his own voice, alongside a slideshow of his many dress-up costumes. The song he chose? "I Don't Look Good Naked Anymore" by The Snake Oil Willie Band.

As for the food, Duncan doesn't mind—he's more focused on making it a fun, humorous event, full of laughter and plenty of beer. He'd love for his two sons and my brother to share funny stories, keeping the atmosphere lighthearted, just the way he would want it.

Now it's your turn:

What's your wish? How do you envision your final act? Take a moment to jot down your thoughts:

_____

_____

_____

_____

There's no right or wrong answer here. Your wish should be as unique as you are. Whether you want a traditional service, a party that rivals New Year's Eve, or something completely out of left field, the choice is yours. This is your story – make the ending unforgettable.

CHAPTER 5:

Selecting a Funeral Home and Funeral Director

Choosing a Reputable Funeral Home

From choreographing your life's grand finale, we pirouette to the backstage crew who'll make it happen – your funeral home and director. Think of this as casting the production team for your posthumous Broadway show. Get it right, and they'll turn your vision into a standing ovation. Get it wrong, and, well... let's just say you don't want your last performance to bomb.

Choosing a funeral home is like dating, but with higher stakes and (hopefully) less ghosting. You're looking for a long-term commitment, even if you won't be around to enjoy it. So how do you swipe right on the perfect match?

First, reputation is king. In the age of internet sleuthing, there's no excuse for not digging up the dirt (pun intended) on potential funeral homes. Yelp reviews, Better Business Bureau ratings, local forums – if there's chatter, listen to it. A funeral home with more skeletons in its closet than a haunted house is a hard pass.

Location, location, location – it's not just for real estate. Unless you're planning a destination funeral (now there's an idea), pick a place that's convenient for your guests. You don't want Aunt Edna getting lost and ending up at a stranger's wake.

Now, let's talk aesthetics. Does the funeral home look like it's stuck in a time warp from 1972? Unless that's your vibe, keep looking. You want a place that reflects your style, not one that makes your guests feel like extras in a bad 70s movie.

Size matters, but bigger isn't always better. A cozy, intimate setting might be perfect for your small gathering, while a grand hall could be ideal for your epic life celebration. Choose a place that fits your guest list like Cinderella's slipper.

Here's a pro tip: Sniff test the place. Literally. A good funeral home should smell neutral, not like they're trying to mask the scent of, well, you know. If it smells like they've bathed in Febreze, run for the hills.

Tech-savviness is crucial in our digital age. Can they livestream your service for far-flung relatives? Do they offer digital guestbooks or memorial websites? If their idea of high-tech is a fax machine, it might be time to look elsewhere.

Flexibility is key. You want a funeral home that's a "yes, and" partner, not a "no, but" dream-crusher. If they balk at your request for a Viking send-off or a disco-themed memorial, keep shopping.

Don't forget to check their license and credentials. A funeral home without proper certification is like a doctor without a medical degree — absolutely terrifying and most likely illegal.

Price transparency is non-negotiable. If their pricing structure is more complicated than quantum physics, that's a red flag. You want a clear, itemized list of costs, not a surprise bill that'll have your family seeing more red than a matador's cape.

Lastly, trust your gut. If something feels off, it probably is. This is your final shindig we're talking about — you deserve a funeral home that gets you, respects your wishes, and isn't just trying to upsell you on a gold-plated casket with surround sound.

Choosing a funeral home isn't just about finding a place to host your farewell party. It's about selecting partners who'll honor your legacy, respect your wishes, and turn your final bow into a show-stopping performance. So choose wisely, choose boldly, and maybe throw in a surprise or two. After all, who says you can't keep them guessing, even from the great beyond?

Questions to Ask When Meeting with a Funeral Director

Now that you've scouted the perfect venue for your grand finale, it's time for the ultimate job interview – grilling the funeral director. This isn't just small talk over coffee; it's your chance to separate the wheat from the chaff, the pros from the posers, the maestros from the meh-stros.

Think of this as speed dating, but instead of finding your soulmate, you're finding someone to handle you. Here's your cheat sheet of questions guaranteed to make any funeral director sweat more than a sinner in church:

1. "What's your refund policy if I decide to come back to life?" Okay, jokes aside, but do ask about their cancellation and refund policies. Life (and death) can be unpredictable.

2. "Can you handle a flash mob of dancing pallbearers?" In all seriousness, inquire about their experience with unique or non-traditional services. You want a director who's a "yes, and" person, not a "no, but" dream-crusher.

3. "What's your stance on biodegradable glitter in the casket?" This quirky question can segue into a discussion about eco-friendly options. It's your chance to gauge their green cred.

4. "If my Uncle Bob insists on singing his off-key rendition of 'My Way', can you provide earplugs for the other guests?" This opens up a conversation about how they

handle family dynamics and special requests.

5.   "What's your hidden fee to corpse ratio?" Cut through the BS and ask for a clear, itemized price list. The last thing you want is your family getting a bill that'll wake the dead (namely, you).

6.   "Can you ensure my ex doesn't crash the funeral and dramatically throw themselves on the casket?" This is your subtle way of asking about security measures and guest management.

7.   "If I want to be buried with my collection of rubber ducks, is that kosher?" Use this to discuss personalization options and any limitations they might have.

8.   "What's your policy on posthumous social media updates?" This leads into a chat about their tech-savviness and digital memorial options.

9.   "Can you guarantee that I'll look less dead and more 'just taking a really long nap'?" This is your cue to discuss their approach to body preparation and presentation.

10.   "If I haunt you for doing a subpar job, what's your ghostbusting policy?" Joke aside, ask about their aftercare services and support for grieving families.

11.   "What's your stance on Viking funerals? Asking for a friend." This opens up a dialogue about alternative burial methods and their willingness to think outside the pine box.

12.   "Can you make me look like I died doing something cooler than binge-watching Netflix?" Use this to segue into a discussion about how they honor the deceased's life story and personality in the service.

A good funeral director won't bat an eye at these questions. They'll appreciate your humor, your thoroughness, and your desire to make your final exit as perfectly "you" as possible.

The right director will match your energy, whether you're planning a solemn affair or a celebration that'll make Mardi Gras look like a tea party. They'll be part event planner, part therapist, part magician — turning your final wishes into a reality show finale worthy of an Emmy.

Now go ahead, ask the tough questions, the weird questions, the questions that'll make them wonder if they should be planning a funeral or a circus. Because in the end, this is your show, and you need a director who can bring your vision to life... even in death.

Understanding the Services Offered by Funeral Homes

After grilling your potential funeral director like a seasoned detective, it's time to decode the menu of services they're offering. Think of a funeral home as a one-stop shop for your grand exit — part event planner, part concierge, and part magician who can make your wildest (final) dreams come true.

Let's peel back the velvet curtain and see what's really on offer:

1. Body Chauffeur Services: They'll pick you up from wherever you decided to make your final bow — hospital, home, or that embarrassing spot where you tripped over your own shoelaces. They're like Uber, but for the no-longer-breathing crowd.

2. Corpse Spa Day: Also known as "preparation services." This is where they'll make you look less "walking dead" and more "just taking a really long nap." Embalming, dressing, hair, and makeup — it's basically the ultimate makeover show, minus the big reveal.

3. Casket Casting: From simple pine boxes to mahogany masterpieces that cost more than your first car, they've got options. Remember, you can't take it with you, but you can sure as hell be buried in it.

4. Venue Virtuosos: Whether you want a traditional chapel service or a beachside bonanza, they'll set the stage for

your final performance.

5. Paperwork Ninjas: Death certificates, permits, obituaries – they'll navigate the red tape jungle so your family doesn't have to. It's like having a personal assistant for the administrative tasks in your afterlife.

6. Funeral Choreography: They'll orchestrate the whole shebang – from directing sobbing relatives to ensuring Uncle Bob doesn't monopolize the eulogy mic.

7. Grief Guidance: Many offer counseling services or can point your loved ones toward support groups. Think of it as emotional GPS for the bereaved.

8. Post-Party Cleanup: Once the last mourner has ugly-cried their way home, they'll handle the flower disposal and venue restoration. No one wants to be stuck doing dishes after their own funeral.

9. Eternal Real Estate Agents: If you're going for the burial route, they can help you pick out prime cemetery real estate. Location, location, location – even in death.

10. Ash Management: For the cremation crowd, they'll handle everything from helping your family decide whether you'll end up on the mantle or being scattered over the Pacific.

11. Digital Afterlife Services: Some offer live streaming for your geographically challenged guests or online memorial pages. Welcome to Death 2.0.

12. Cortège Coordination: They'll line up the funeral procession like a boss, ensuring you make your last journey in style. It's like a parade, but with less confetti and more sobbing.

13. Flower Power Management: From casket sprays to standing wreaths, they'll make sure your service is blooming lovely.

14. International Repatriation: If you decide to kick the bucket abroad, they'll help bring you home. It's like a really somber version of "Around the World in 80 Days."

Not all funeral homes are created equal. Some might offer bare-bones services (pun intended), while others provide everything short of resurrecting you. The key is finding the right fit for your final bow.

And here's the plot twist – you don't have to use all their services. Mix and match, customize, or even DIY some aspects if you're feeling crafty. Your funeral is like a cosmic buffet - take what you want, leave what you don't.

Understanding these services isn't just about knowing what's on offer. It's about empowering yourself (or your loved ones) to create a send-off that's as unique as your fingerprint. So go ahead, pick and choose, haggle and customize. After all, this is one party you definitely don't want to miss... even though you will.

CHAPTER 6:

Funeral Planning Checklist

A Step-by-Step Guide to Planning a Funeral

From casting your funeral's dream team, we're now rolling out the red carpet for your grand production. Ladies and gentlemen, it's showtime – your funeral planning checklist is about to take center stage!

Think of this as your Oscar-winning script, your magnum opus, your mic-drop moment. It's the roadmap that'll turn your final bow from a chaotic circus act into a perfectly choreographed performance. So, grab your director's hat, and let's make funeral planning history!

Act I: The Immediate Aftermath (0-24 hours post-curtain call)

1. Make the announcement: Time to break the news. It's like dropping a plot twist, but with more tears and fewer gasps.
2. Notify the VIPs: Family, close friends, and your goldfish (okay, maybe not the goldfish).
3. Engage your funeral director: Your chosen maestro of memorial services springs into action.
4. Arrange transportation for your earthly vessel: Your final limo ride awaits.

Act II: Setting the Stage (24-72 hours post-final bow)

1. Choose your funeral's genre: Traditional tear-jerker or avant-garde celebration?
2. Pick your venue: Church, funeral home, or that karaoke bar you loved?
3. Decide on your body's fate: Burial or cremation? It's your last big decision, no pressure.
4. Select your forever outfit: What would you wear to meet the universe?
5. Choose your flower entourage: Unless you prefer donations to the "Send My Ex to Mars" fund.

Act III: The Supporting Cast (3-5 days before the main event)

1. Write your life's highlight reel (obituary): Make it Oscar-worthy.
2. Cast your pallbearers: Choose wisely, they're literally carrying you out.
3. Select your eulogy all-stars: Who can sum up your life without putting everyone to sleep?
4. Plan your soundtrack: From Mozart to Metallica, make it yours.
5. Design your program: It's your last chance to be an editor-in-chief.

Act IV: The Finishing Touches (1-2 days before showtime)

1. Arrange the after-party (reception): Because who doesn't want food after an emotional rollercoaster?
2. Prepare your guest list: Yes, even that cousin you haven't spoken to in years.
3. Coordinate transportation for the living: Nobody should get lost on their way to say goodbye.
4. Do a tech run: Mics, music, slideshow - make sure it's all ready to roll.

5.   Prepare for international guests: Death doesn't check passports, but customs does.

Act V: The Main Event (Show day)

1.   Final venue check: Is everything in its right place? Are the tissues strategically placed?
2.   Coordinate with your funeral director: Your day-of wedding planner, but for... you know.
3.   Receive guests: Well, not you personally, but you get the idea.
4.   Execute the service: Lights, camera, funeral action!
5.   Lead the procession: Your final parade. Make it count.

Post-Credits Scene: The Aftermath

1.   Thank your guests: Gratitude never goes out of style, even post-mortem.
2.   Collect and distribute memorial gifts: Your last round of party favors.
3.   Order death certificates: Because bureaucracy doesn't end with death.
4.   Navigate the paperwork maze: Wills, accounts, subscriptions — it's time to tidy up.

This isn't just a to-do list. It's the blueprint for your legacy's last hurrah. Each checkbox is a brushstroke on the masterpiece of your memory. So, tailor it, twist it, make it as unique as that birthmark on your left toe.

Your funeral isn't just an event; it's the final chapter of your life's bestseller. Make it a page-turner, a tear-jerker, a laugh-out-loud comedy - whatever fits your story. Because in the end, this checklist isn't about death. It's about celebrating the vibrant, messy and beautiful life you lived.

Now, grab your pen (or quill, or digital stylus — we don't judge), and start plotting. Your grand finale awaits, and darling, it's going to be legendary.

Making Arrangements for the Funeral service, Burial or Cremation, Obituary, and more

From your Oscar-worthy checklist, we're zooming in on the nitty-gritty details of your grand finale. It's time to roll up your sleeves and dive into the art of funeral arranging. This isn't just planning; it's orchestrating a symphony of memories, tears, and maybe a few inappropriate giggles.

Funeral Service: The Main Event. Think of this as your last party – and you're the guest of honor who can't complain about the music. Will it be a solemn affair or a celebration that makes Mardi Gras look tame? Choose a tone that screams "you." Religious? Secular? A mix of both with a dash of stand-up comedy? The sky (or perhaps the ground) is the limit.

Location, location, location! Church, funeral home, your favorite park, or that dive bar where you met your spouse – pick a place that tells your story. Remember, this is your last chance to get everyone together in one room without having to cook for them.

Cremation vs. Burial: The Ultimate Heat vs. Treat Decision Cremation: Going out in a blaze of glory. Quick, efficient, and you get to spend eternity in an urn that matches your decor. Plus, you can finally fulfill your dream of being scattered somewhere exotic or sitting on your grandson's mantle next to his participation trophies.

Burial: The classic choice for those who want their own piece of real estate, even in the afterlife. It's like moving into a very small, very permanent studio apartment. Choose your plot wisely – it's the longest lease you'll ever sign.

Green Burial: For those who want to return to nature faster than a hippie at Woodstock. No embalming, no fancy casket – just you and Mother Earth in a beautiful, biodegradable embrace.

The Obituary: Your Life's Highlight Reel. This is your last chance to brag, so make it count. Born, died, and in between? That's just the outline. Fill it with the juicy bits - your achievements, your quirks, that time you won a hot dog eating contest. Make it so good that people will fight over the newspaper clippings.

Pro tip: Write it yourself. It's like leaving a cheat sheet for your family and denying your nemesis the chance to have the last word.

The Guest List: Your Final Social Circle. Curate this list like it's the Met Gala of the afterlife. Family? Obviously. Friends? Sure. That guy who owes you money? Maybe he'll feel guilty and pay your kids. Your ex? Only if you're feeling particularly forgiving (or want to give them one last chance to see what they missed).

The Soundtrack: Your Life's Playlist. From processional to recessional, pick tunes that make people say, "Yep, that's definitely them." Classical, rock, or your weird obsession with polka – let your musical freak flag fly one last time. Just remember, if you choose "Highway to Hell," you might give your religious aunt a heart attack.

Flowers or Charitable Donations: Blooms or Booms? Flowers are nice, but they die (ironic, isn't it?). Consider asking for donations to your favorite charity instead. It's like giving the world one last gift, proving you're generous even when you're not around to get the tax write-off.

The Dress Code: Your Last Fashion Statement. All black is so last season. Why not request Hawaiian shirts, superhero costumes, or formal wear with sneakers? It's your party; you can dress code if you want to.

Arranging your funeral isn't just about checking boxes. It's about crafting an experience that's as unique as your fingerprint, as memorable as your laugh, and as special as that mole on your left cheek that you always thought looked like Elvis.

This is your final performance, your last hurrah, your ultimate mic drop. So make it spectacular, make it meaningful, make it "you". Because in the end, this isn't just about saying goodbye - it's about celebrating the one-of-a-kind story that was your life.

Now go forth and plan. Your standing ovation awaits!

Tips for Creating a Meaningful and Personalized Funeral Ceremony

From crafting your life's highlight reel, we're now fine-tuning the details to ensure your final bow is as uniquely "you" as that embarrassing tattoo you got in college. Creating a meaningful, personalized funeral ceremony isn't just about avoiding a cookie-cutter send-off; it's about turning your farewell into a standing ovation-worthy performance that would make Broadway jealous.

1. **Theme it like you mean it**: Why settle for somber when you can go full thematic? Love to travel? Transform the venue into a globe-trotting adventure. Gardening enthusiast? Turn it into a bloom-filled botanical garden. Your funeral should be more "you" than your Facebook profile ever was.

2. **Curate a "Memory Museum"**: Create a gallery of your life's greatest hits. Embarrassing childhood photos, that trophy from the hot dog eating contest, the half-finished novel you swore you'd write. Let your guests take a walk through the museum of You.

3. **Soundtrack your send-off**: Ditch the organ dirges for a playlist that screams "you". From classical to classic rock, K-pop to country, make them bob their heads even as they dab their eyes. Bonus points if you can make your straight-laced uncle accidentally headbang.

4. **Dress code**: Memory Lane Edition. Instead of black, why not ask guests to wear your favorite color? Or clothes that remind them of you? Picture a sea of Hawaiian shirts, superhero tees, or that specific shade of purple you always claimed brought out your eyes.

5. **Interactive remembrance**: Set up stations where guests can share memories. A giant canvas for written messages, a video booth for teary (or hilarious)

tributes, or a puzzle where each guest adds a piece. It's like a yearbook signing, but with more emotional weight and less "H.A.G.S."

6. **Personalized party favors**: Send them home with a piece of you. Packets of your famous chili recipe, a mini version of your signature cocktail, or seedlings of your favorite flower. It's your last chance to be the host with the most.

7. **Ritual with a twist**: Create a unique ritual that encapsulates your spirit. A collective toast with your favorite drink, a balloon release (biodegradable, of course - you're dead, not an environmental terrorist), or a massive group hug that would make the Guinness Book of Records weep.

8. **Tech-savvy tributes**: Use technology to bridge distances and timelines. A hologram message from you, a VR experience of your favorite places, or a livestream for those who can't attend. It's like Black Mirror, but with more tears and less dystopia.

9. **Humor**, because why not? Inject some laughter into the tears. A standup routine about your life, a blooper reel of your most embarrassing moments, or a roast (you can't fight back now, can you?). Remember, it's only too soon if you say it is.

10. **Symbolic send-off**: End with a bang, not a whimper. A sky lantern release, a collective howl at the moon, or everyone planting a tree in your memory. Give them a final moment that's more powerful than a triple shot espresso.

11. **Open mic memories**: Turn your funeral into a live show. Encourage guests to share stories, from heartwarming to hilariously embarrassing. It's like a roast, a tribute, and a therapy session all rolled into one.

12. **Sensory Overload** (In a Good Way) Engage all the senses. Your favorite scents wafting through the air, a touch station with textures you loved, a tasting menu of your favorite snacks. Make it a full-body experience

that would put 4D movies to shame.

Keep in mind, this isn't just a funeral; it's the after-party for the epic event that was your life. Make it so engaging, so "you", so unforgettable that people leave thinking, "Damn, I wish I'd known them better in life." Your funeral should be the hottest ticket in town, the event of the season, the talk of the afterlife.

So go ahead, plan a send-off that's so perfectly "you", it'll have people checking their pulse to make sure they're still alive. After all, if you can't go out with a bang, what's the point of going out at all?

Jenni's stepmother Joan, an amazing person, died not so long ago at 92 and created a book page marker that had words of wisdom. Jenni loves opening a book she is currently reading and seeing her beautiful face and wants to share her message:

No one dies, but we change focus and depart the physical "Container".

There is no death, only arrivals and departures, transitions and eternal change.

'With you always'

Keep me in your thoughts. I will always live through my family and through my life which has been so full and so happy as Mother, Joan, Partner & Wife, Jana and Great Jana.

The more you do, The more you are, The more you give, The more you get.

I am so grateful for all my loved ones' presence in my life.

CHAPTER 7:

Supporting Loved Ones Through the Funeral Process

Helping Children Cope with Loss and the Funeral Process

From orchestrating your personalized grand finale, we pivot to the pint-sized members of your audience. Yes, it's time to tackle the delicate art of helping kids navigate the funeral funhouse - minus the fun, plus a whole lot of confusing emotions.

Welcome to "Grief: The Kiddie Edition." It's like explaining quantum physics to a goldfish, but with more tears and existential questions.

First things first: Kids aren't mini-adults. Their grief comes in child-sized portions, served with a side of bewilderment and the occasional inappropriate giggle. They're emotional ninjas, switching from sobbing to asking for ice cream in 0.5 seconds flat.

Honesty is your best policy. Sugar-coating death is like putting sprinkles on a broccoli sundae - it doesn't make it any more palatable. Use clear, simple language. "Grandpa died" is better than "Grandpa went to sleep forever." Unless you want your kid to develop a crippling fear of bedtime.

Encourage questions, even the weird ones. "Does Grandma poop in heaven?" Congratulations, you're now a theologian and a potty expert. Roll with it. Their curiosity is their way of processing, no matter how bizarre the inquiry.

Involve them in the funeral planning. Let them pick a flower for the casket or choose a photo for display. It gives them a sense of control in a situation where everything feels out of control. Just maybe veto the suggestion of a bouncy castle at the cemetery.

Explain what they'll see and hear at the funeral. It's like giving them a sneak preview of the world's saddest movie. Prepare them for tears, hugs, and that one relative who always wails dramatically. Knowledge is power, even when it's about Aunt Edna's theatrical sobbing.

Create a comfort kit for the service. A favorite stuffed animal, a stress ball, or a small photo album. It's their emotional survival pack for the funeral frontlines.

Give them a role. Maybe they can hand out programs or help arrange flowers. It's not child labor if it's therapeutic, right?

Allow for their unique expressions of grief. If they want to draw pictures of the deceased or write them letters, go for it. It's better than them expressing grief by flushing your keys down the toilet. (Speaking from experience? Maybe.)

Watch for signs of trouble. Regression, aggression, or the sudden belief they're a reincarnated pirate captain – all of these can be signs they're struggling. Time to call in the child psychology cavalry.

Remember, their grief isn't a straight line; it's more like a drunk squirrel's path through a maze. They might seem fine one minute and fall apart the next. Flexibility is key. Be prepared to switch from consoling hugger to tickle monster at a moment's notice.

Don't forget the power of routine. In a world turned upside down, knowing that Tuesday is still taco night can be incredibly comforting. Death may have changed everything, but Mr. Snuggles the bear still needs his nightly hug.

Lastly, take care of yourself. You can't pour from an empty cup, especially when that cup is supposed to be filled with emotional support and impromptu dinosaur facts (because kids will ask about dinosaurs at the most inappropriate times).

Helping kids through grief isn't about having all the answers. It's about being there, being honest, and being okay with not being okay. It's messy, it's unpredictable, and sometimes it involves explaining why we can't actually send Grandpa's ashes to space in fireworks (thanks for that idea, little Timmy).

Remember, you're not just helping them cope with loss; you're teaching them how to navigate life's toughest moments. And who knows? Maybe their resilience and unexpected questions will help you process your own grief. After all, nothing puts things into perspective quite like a 5-year-old solemnly informing you that Grandpa is now best friends with dinosaurs in heaven.

Communicating Effectively with Family and Friends

From guiding mini-mourners through the grief maze, we're now tackling the Herculean task of adult communication. Ah yes, the delicate art of talking to grown-ups about death without causing a family feud that would make the Hatfields and McCoys look like a tea party.

Welcome to "Funeral Talk: Where Every Conversation is a Potential Minefield". It's like a high-stakes game of Telephone, but instead of funny misunderstandings, you get tears, arguments about Grandma's china, and that one cousin who suddenly thinks he's the reincarnation of the deceased. Fun times!

First rule of Grief Club: Everyone grieves differently. Your stoic brother might look like he's auditioning for a role of a statue while your drama queen sister is reenacting scenes from a telenovela. Neither is wrong; they're just tuned to different emotional radio stations.

Clarity is your new best friend. This isn't the time for flowery language or beating around the bush. "Dad died" works better than "Father has embarked on his eternal journey to the great beyond." Unless, of course, your family communicates exclusively in poetry. In which case, sonnet away!

Timing is everything. Dropping the "Hey, we need to decide on Dad's burial outfit" bomb during Thanksgiving dinner is a surefire way to turn stuffing into ammunition. Choose your moments wisely, preferably when everyone's sober and not wielding sharp utensils.

Listen more than you speak. Sometimes people just need to verbally vomit their feelings. Your job? Be the emotional barf bag. It's not glamorous, but it's necessary. And hey, at least it's metaphorical vomit. Silver linings, people!

Be the information hub. Create a group chat, email thread, or carrier pigeon network (for the tech-averse relatives) to keep everyone in the loop. It prevents the dreaded "Why am I always the last to know?" syndrome.

Delegate like a boss. Aunt Martha's great at organizing? Put her in charge of the photo displays. Uncle Bob's a numbers whiz? He's now the budget guru. It gives everyone a sense of purpose and prevents you from turning into a funeral-planning Gollum, hissing "My precious" at the memorial program drafts.

Handle the drama llamas with care. There's always one relative who thrives on chaos. Acknowledge their feelings, then gently steer them towards productive tasks. "I hear you're upset about the flower choices. Why don't you oversee the reception menu instead?" Distraction: It's not just for toddlers anymore!

Be the conflict referee. When tensions rise (and oh, they will), be the voice of reason. "I'm sure Mom wouldn't want us fighting over her cookie jar. How about we take turns displaying it?" Compromise: It's like yoga for relationships, but with less stretching and more eye-rolling.

Remember the power of touch. Sometimes a hug says more than words ever could. Just make sure you're hugging the right person. Accidentally embracing the funeral director could lead to some awkward moments.

Don't forget the out-of-towners. Keep them in the loop and give them tasks they can do remotely. They'll feel included, and you'll have someone to blame when something goes wrong. "Sorry, the typo in the obituary was Cousin Sarah's fault. She's in Australia, you know."

Humor is your secret weapon. Used wisely, it can defuse tension and bring light to dark moments. Just maybe avoid the "I see dead people" jokes. There's a time and a place, and this ain't it.

Above all, be kind - to others and to yourself. You're all fumbling through this together, like a bunch of emotional toddlers learning to walk. There will be falls, bumps, and probably some tears. But with patience, love, and maybe a bit of wine (for the adults, obviously), you'll make it through.

Effective communication during this time isn't about being perfect. It's about being present, being honest, and occasionally being the person who orders pizza when everyone's too emotionally drained to cook. In the grand tapestry of grief, sometimes the strongest threads are woven with shared silences, awkward laughs, and the mutual understanding that this whole "dealing with death" thing is weird, hard, and somehow, eventually, okay.

Finding Supportive Resources for Grief

From navigating the minefield of family communication, we're now on a quest for the Holy Grail of grief support. Welcome to "Grief Resources: Because Sometimes Ice Cream and Netflix Aren't Enough."

Picture this: You've mastered the art of not strangling Aunt Edna for asking if you're "over it yet", but your emotional gas tank is running on fumes. It's time to call in the cavalry, the grief gurus, the sorrow specialists. In short, it's time to find your tribe of fellow heart-hurt humans.

First stop: Therapy Town. Population: You and a box of tissues. Finding a grief counselor is like dating, but instead of swiping right on potential soulmates, you're looking for someone who won't mind if you ugly-cry for 50 minutes straight. Shop around, because not all therapists are created equal. Some specialize in grief, others in making you realize your childhood hamster's death is why you can't commit to relationships. Choose wisely.

Next up: Support Groups — where misery doesn't just love company, it forms a book club with it. These groups come in all flavors: Young Widows, Parents Who've Lost Children, People Whose Cats Lived Longer Than Their Spouses. Find your niche. It's like Finding Nemo, but instead of fish, you're searching for people who understand why you burst into tears at the sight of your loved one's favorite cereal.

Online forums: For when you need support at 3 AM because grief apparently doesn't believe in business hours. These digital gathering spaces are like the Wild West of emotions — raw, unfiltered, and occasionally spelling-challenged. But they're there, 24/7, ready to virtually hold your hand through the dark nights of the soul.

Books: Because sometimes the best advice comes from dead trees. From self-help guides to memoirs of loss, there's a veritable library of "I've been there, and it sucks, but you'll be okay" waiting for you. Pro tip: Audiobooks are great for when your eyes are too puffy from crying to actually read.

Apps: Yes, there's an app for grief. Several, in fact. From guided meditations to digital memory books, your smartphone can now be your pocket-sized grief guru. Just don't mix up your grief app with your dating app. Telling your Tinder match about your complex bereavement process is a surefire way to ensure you'll be grieving your love life too.

Religious or Spiritual Resources: If you're the spiritual type, your local religious leader might be a fountain of wisdom. Or at least they'll have some really good quotes about the afterlife. Bonus: Most places of worship come with a built-in community and often have casseroles. Never underestimate the healing power of a good casserole.

Volunteer Organizations: Sometimes, the best way to heal is to help. Organizations that support causes your loved one cared about can be a beautiful way to honor their memory and find purpose in your pain. It's like emotional alchemy – turning your grief into gold (or at least into something that doesn't feel like it's eating you alive).

Creative Outlets: Art therapy, writing workshops, interpretive dance classes – find a way to externalize your internal chaos. Who knows? Your grief journal might become the next bestseller, or your interpretive dance could go viral on TikTok. Stranger things have happened in the name of healing.

Nature: Never underestimate the therapeutic power of screaming your lungs out in the middle of a forest. It's free, it's cathartic, and the trees are excellent listeners. Just maybe warn any nearby hikers first.

Finding support isn't a one-size-fits-all endeavor. It's more like trying on emotional outfits until you find what feels right. Some days you might need the structure of therapy, others the chaos of a paint-throwing art class. The key is to keep reaching out, keep trying, and remembering that needing help doesn't make you weak – it makes you human.

In the end, the best resource might be a combination of all of the above, sprinkled with a healthy dose of patience for yourself. Grief isn't a problem to be solved; it's an experience to be lived through. So live it, with all the support you can gather, knowing that one day, you'll be the one offering a hand (or a casserole) to someone else just starting this wild, heart-wrenching journey.

CHAPTER 8:

Preparing for the Future

Creating an End-of-Life Plan

From finding your grief support dream team, we're now switching gears to become the architects of our own grand finale. Welcome to "End-of-Life Planning: Because Winging It Is So Last Century".

Picture this: You're the director of the most important movie of your life – the one that plays after the credits roll. Creating an end-of-life plan is like writing, producing, and directing your final blockbuster. And trust me, you want this to be more "Citizen Kane" than "Sharknado 5."

First on the agenda: The Legal Tango. Time to waltz with wills, two-step with trusts, and foxtrot with power of attorney documents. It's a complicated dance, but it beats leaving your family to freestyle their way through probate court. Remember, without a will, the state becomes your posthumous party planner, and let's face it, bureaucrats aren't known for their event planning skills.

Next up: The Medical Mambo. Advance directives are your way of saying, "If I'm vegging harder than a head of lettuce, please don't keep me as a science experiment." Living wills and healthcare proxies ensure your wishes are respected, even when you're too busy imitating Sleeping Beauty to voice them yourself.

Now, for the main event: The Funeral Foxtrot. This is where you get to choreograph your final bow. Burial or cremation? Traditional service or a rave at the local pub? Maybe you want your ashes shot into space or turned into a diamond. The sky (or the ground) is the limit. Just remember, if you choose something too outlandish, your family might think you've been replaced by an alien body snatcher.

Don't forget the Financial Flamenco. This spicy number involves organizing your assets, debts, and accounts. It's like playing Monopoly, but with real money and actual consequences. Leave clear instructions, unless you want your kids fighting over your collection of rare Beanie Babies like it's the Holy Grail.

The Digital Cha-Cha is next on our dance card. In this age of online everything, you need a plan for your digital afterlife. Passwords, social media accounts, that embarrassing blog from 2005 - all need to be addressed. Decide who gets access to what, or risk having your Facebook profile turned into a digital shrine that posts Minion memes for all eternity.

Now, for the Emotional Salsa. This is where you spice things up with personal messages, ethical wills, or video recordings. It's your chance to dispense final words of wisdom, reveal family secrets, or finally admit it was you who ate the last cookie in 1987. Make it count — it's your last chance to have the last word.

The Spiritual Samba lets you address any religious or philosophical wishes. Whether you want a traditional religious service, a secular celebration of life, or a Viking funeral (check local laws first), this is your moment to shine. Or burn. Whatever floats your proverbial boat.

Then it's time for the Legacy Lambada. How do you want to be remembered? Scholarships, charitable donations, a bench in the park with a plaque that says "I told you I was sick"? This is your opportunity to leave a mark on the world that lasts longer than your Instagram posts.

Creating an end-of-life plan isn't about being morbid. It's about taking control, easing burdens, and ensuring your final performance is standing ovation worthy. It's a gift to your loved ones, sparing them from playing a high-stakes game of "Guess What Dad Wanted" while they're trying to remember how to breathe without you.

Discussing Funeral Wishes with Loved Ones

After scripting your life's finale, you'll now face the ultimate challenge: Actually telling people about it. Welcome to "Funeral Wish Discussions: Where 'Pass the Salt' Becomes 'Pass the Urn Catalog'".

Picture this: You've meticulously planned your grand exit, right down to the choreographed dance number at your cremation (you always were a "Burn, Baby, Burn" fan). But your masterpiece is still a secret, locked away like that diary you kept in middle school. It's time for the big reveal, and no, you can't just leave it as a surprise ending.

First things first: Timing is everything. Blurting out "I want my ashes mixed with glitter and shot out of a cannon" over Thanksgiving dinner might not be the best approach. Unless, of course, you're trying to see how many people can choke on a turkey simultaneously. Choose a calm moment, preferably when everyone's sober and not wielding sharp objects.

Location, location, location. Pick a comfortable, private space for this chat. The living room? Perfect. The local pub? Could work, especially if liquid courage is needed. The family group chat? Absolutely not. Some things are too important for emojis and "k" responses.

Start with the why. Explain that this isn't a morbid obsession but an act of love. You're not auditioning for a vampire role; you're trying to make their lives easier when you're busy pushing up daisies. It's like meal prepping, but for your afterlife.

Be prepared for a range of reactions. Some might be relieved you've taken charge. Others might act like you've just announced you're leaving Earth to colonize Mars. Patience is key. Remember, you've had time to think this through; they're getting it sprung on them like a pop quiz in existential studies.

Use humor as your secret weapon. It's the spoonful of sugar that helps the mortality medicine go down. "I've decided on cremation. It's my last chance to have a smoking hot body!" Just maybe avoid the "knock-knock" jokes. There's a time and a place, and this ain't it.

Be specific, but flexible. Share your wishes clearly, but be open to input. Maybe your plan to have your ashes turned into a firework display isn't feasible. Or legal. Be willing to compromise, unless it's about Aunt Edna giving the eulogy. Some things are non-negotiable.

Encourage questions. Even the weird ones. "Do you want your cat to attend the funeral?", "Can we dress you up as Elvis?" Answer honestly. This is your show, after all. If you want your cat there in a custom-made tuxedo, say so.

Address the elephant in the room: Money. Funerals can be pricier than a small island. Be upfront about your financial plans. Are you setting aside funds? Expecting them to chip in? Planning to haunt the richest relative until they cough up the cash? Clarity is kindness.

Don't forget the practical details. Where are your important documents? Who gets your collection of rare Pog slammers? What's the password to your secret Twitter account where you've been posing as a cantankerous sea captain? These details matter.

Be prepared to revisit the conversation. This isn't a one-and-done deal. As shocking as it may be, people might need time to process the fact that you want your headstone to read "I told you I was sick".

End with love. Remind them that this planning isn't about your death; it's about making your love for them extend beyond your expiration date. It's your final gift, wrapped in legal papers and sealed with embalming fluid.

Remember, discussing your funeral wishes isn't just about logistics. It's an opportunity for meaningful connections, shared laughs, and maybe a few tears. It's a chance to reflect on life, love, and the unbridled joy of planning one last party – even if you'll be the only guest who can't complain about the music.

So go ahead, break the ice. Share your plans. Let them in on the secret. After all, your farewell party is going to be legendary – it'd be a shame not to give them a sneak preview.

Reviewing and Updating Funeral Plans Regularly

Now that you've spilled the beans about your desire to have your ashes turned into a disco ball, it's time for the thrilling sequel: "Funeral Plan Reviews: Because Even Death Needs Updates".

Think of this as your afterlife software. Just like how your phone nags you about system updates, your funeral plans need regular check-ins. Why? Because life changes faster than fashion trends, and what seemed like a great idea at 30 might seem utterly ridiculous at 60 (look at you, planning to be buried in a KISS costume all those years ago).

Set a schedule. Yearly? On your birthday? Every time Apple releases a new iPhone? Pick a time that works for you. Just don't wait for signs from the beyond. By then, it'll be a tad too late.

Start with the basics. Are you still dead set on cremation, or has that cave diving hobby made you reconsider a burial at sea? Maybe that plan to have your body donated to science needs revisiting now that you've discovered your new passion for full-body tattoos.

Check your supporting cast. Is the person you chose as your healthcare proxy still alive? Still talking to you? Still sane enough to make decisions more complex than choosing a Netflix show? Time for a potential recast.

Review your financial strategy. Has inflation turned your funeral fund into enough money to maybe buy a nice floral arrangement and a sympathy card? Time to adjust those numbers, unless you're planning on a DIY cardboard box burial.

Examine your digital legacy plan. Remember MySpace? No? Exactly. As platforms come and go, make sure your digital executor isn't tasked with managing your no-longer-existent Friendster account.

Assess your music choices. That song you chose for your funeral might have seemed deep and meaningful once, but do you really want your final soundtrack to be "Who Let the Dogs Out"? (Unless you're a veterinarian, in which case, carry on.)

Reevaluate your final resting outfit. That leisure suit might have been the height of fashion when you first made your plans, but let's be real — no one looks good in polyester for eternity.

Check local laws and regulations. Maybe that plan to be buried in your backyard is no longer legal. Or perhaps new green burial options have opened up, allowing you to fulfill your lifelong dream of becoming tree friendly, you can be as tall as you always claimed to be on your driver's license!).

Consider technological advancements. Who knows? By the time you kick the bucket, we might have the option to upload our consciousness to the cloud. "Funeral or system upgrade" might become the new "burial or cremation."

Reflect on your legacy goals. Has your perspective on what you want to leave behind changed? Maybe that plan to donate your body to science has evolved into a desire to have your skeleton displayed in a local haunted house. Hey, no judgment here.

Update your notification list. New friends, estranged relatives, that barista who always remembers your complicated coffee order — your "who to tell" list probably needs some tweaking.

Review your ethical will. Have your values, life lessons, or terrible dad jokes evolved? Update that letter to your descendants. Future generations deserve your most recent pearls of wisdom (and the latest version of that story about how you walked uphill both ways to school).

Remember, updating your funeral plans isn't just about logistics. It's a chance to reflect on your life, your growth, and your ever-evolving taste in farewell party themes. It's an opportunity to ensure that your final bow is as authentic and current as your latest social media profile picture (hopefully with fewer filters).

So, set those reminders, dust off those documents, and dive into the thrilling world of funeral plan updates. Because the only thing worse than a poorly planned funeral is a poorly planned funeral that's also woefully outdated. After all, you may be dead, but your plans should be anything but fossilized.

CHAPTER 9:

Honoring Your Loved One's Memory

Ways to Commemorate The Life of the Deceased after the Funeral.

Now that you've updated your funeral playlist to exclude one-hit wonders, we're now stepping into the realm of "Life After Death: No, Not the Tupac Album." Welcome to the art of keeping memories alive when the star of the show has taken their final bow.

Commemorating a loved one isn't just about dusty photos and somber candlelight vigils. It's about injecting their essence into the world like a spiritual Red Bull, giving life wings long after they've flown the coop.

First up: The Annual Day of Awesome. Pick a day — their birthday, death day, or that time they accidentally set the kitchen on fire making toast — and turn it into a celebration. Eat their favorite foods, watch their beloved movies, or recreate their signature dance moves. It's like Thanksgiving, but with 100% more "remember when" stories and potentially embarrassing photo albums.

For the tech-savvy: Create a digital shrine. A website, social media page, or even a holographic AI (hey, the future is now) dedicated to their memory. Just maybe avoid the chatbot option unless you want Grandma's digital ghost accidentally learning millennial slang and asking if she's still "lit."

Get your hands dirty with a memorial garden. Plant their favorite flowers, or go full circle of life and use their ashes to fertilize a tree. Nothing says "I remember you" quite like cursing their name every time you have to weed their posthumous petunias.

For the artistic souls: Commission a piece of art. A portrait, sculpture, or interpretive dance routine — whatever floats your creative boat. Just maybe skip the life-size ice sculpture unless you're into very temporary memorials.

Establish a scholarship or charity in their name. It's like having a kid without the diaper changes and 3 AM feedings. Their legacy lives on, making the world a better place, one good deed at a time. Plus, it's tax-deductible. Win-win!

For the foodies: Create a signature dish or drink in their honor. Was Dad famous for his chili? Did Grandma have a secret martini recipe? Immortalize it. Just be prepared for the family arguments about who makes it "the right way".

Adventure seekers, listen up: Take a memorial trip. Visit their favorite places or tick off destinations from their bucket list. It's like "Eat, Pray, Love," but with a ghostly tour guide.

Start a tradition of random acts of kindness in their memory. Pay for a stranger's coffee, volunteer at their favorite charity, or help little old ladies cross the street. Just don't go full superhero — capes are hard to pull off unless you're Batman.

For the sentimental types: Create memory boxes for family members. Fill them with photos, trinkets and handwritten notes. It's like a time capsule, but without the risk of future archaeologists misinterpreting your loved one's collection of troll dolls.

Tech wizards, unite: Develop an app or game based on their life or interests. "Grandpa's Fishing Adventures" or "Aunt Sally's Baking Bonanza" could be the next Angry Birds. Or at least a fun way to waste time during family gatherings.

For the musically inclined: Compile a playlist of their favorite songs or ones that remind you of them. It's like a mixtape for the afterlife. Just maybe avoid playing it at full volume at 2 AM unless you want to join them sooner than planned.

Commemorating someone isn't about perfection. It's about keeping their spirit alive in ways that would make them smile, roll their eyes, or say, "What in tarnation are you doing?" It's about turning grief into celebration, tears into laughter, and memories into living tributes.

So go forth and commemorate. Make it weird, make it wonderful, make it them. Because as long as we remember, as long as we celebrate, they're never really gone. They're just waiting in the wings for their eternal encore.

CONCLUSION

Creating a Lasting Tribute (memorial services, monuments, charitable donations etc.)

From annual celebrations of quirkiness to digital shrines, we're now crafting the ultimate mic drop of remembrance. Welcome to "Eternal Echoes: Making Sure They're Remembered Long After the Potato Salad at the Wake Has Gone Bad."

Memorial services aren't just for the day of the funeral. Think of them as greatest hits concerts, but instead of old rock stars reliving their glory days, it's you and your crew belting out the best memories of your dearly departed. Annual services keep the memory fresh, like a perpetual "This Is Your Life" rerun, minus the cheesy host and canned laughter.

Monuments aren't just for pharaohs anymore. From traditional headstones to avant-garde sculptures, the options are as varied as your loved one's Netflix queue. Want a QR code that links to their life story? Done. A bench in their favorite park with a plaque that says, "I'm not lazy, I'm dead"? Morbidly delightful. Just remember, whatever you choose will be there for a long time, so maybe reconsider that emoji headstone.

Charitable donations in their name? It's like franchising their goodwill. Set up a foundation, fund a scholarship, or donate to their favorite cause. It's the gift that keeps on giving, turning your loved one into a posthumous philanthropist. Who knows? Maybe little Timmy will cure cancer thanks to the "Don't Eat Yellow Snow" memorial science scholarship.

Now, let's talk brass tacks (or should that be brass urns?):

Your Grand Finale Cheat Sheet

Venue: Choose wisely. Church, beach, or monster truck rally – pick a place that screams "them". Just maybe avoid anywhere with an open bar if your family's known for turning grief into impromptu WWE matches.

Soundtrack: Curate a playlist that's "more them" than their browser history. From classical to death metal, make those speakers sing their life's soundtrack. Just maybe fade out before that questionable Europop phase they went through in the '90s starts to play.

Speakers: Choose wisely, like you're casting for the Oscars of eulogies. Mix tear-jerkers with laugh-inducers. Aim for an emotional roller coaster that leaves everyone feeling like they've just watched a Pixar movie – thoroughly wrung out but oddly uplifted.

Photo Album: Not just any photos – we're talking the "greatest hits" of their life. Baby photos, awkward teen years, that time they thought frosted tips were a good idea. Create a visual journey that's part comedy, part "aww," and 100% them.

Pallbearers: Pick a squad strong enough to carry a coffin and emotionally sturdy enough not to turn it into a crowd-surfing situation. This isn't Coachella; it's a funeral. Although... no, let's stick with dignity here.

After-Party: Because "reception" sounds too much like a dental appointment. Make it a celebration that would have your loved one FOMO-ing in the afterlife. Serve their favorite foods, play their beloved games, tell their best (and worst) jokes. It's like a birthday party, but with more black outfits and socially acceptable day-drinking.

Menu: Forget bland funeral potatoes. Serve up their favorite dishes. Did they love sushi? Set up a raw bar. Were they a burger aficionado? Gourmet slider station it is. Their last supper should be so good it has people wondering if it's inappropriate to ask for seconds.

The Final Destination: Cremation or burial, it's the ultimate "where are they now?" moment

For the burial crowd: Pick a spot they'd actually want to spend eternity in. Scenic views? Great. Next to that cousin they always argued with? Maybe not.

For the ashes-to-ashes gang: The world's your oyster (urn?). Scatter them somewhere meaningful, turn them into a diamond, shoot them into space, or divide them up so everyone gets a piece (literally). Just check local laws first — no one wants to be arrested for illegal ash-dumping.

As we wrap up this journey through the land of the living planning for the land of the not-so-living, remember: this isn't just about saying goodbye. It's about crafting a hello to a new way of remembering. It's turning "The End" into "To Be Continued," because as long as we remember, as long as we celebrate, the story never really ends.

Your loved one's life was a bestseller. Make sure the epilogue is just as gripping. Create a lasting tribute that has people talking for generations, not because it was perfect, but because it was perfectly them. After all, life's too short for boring endings, and the afterlife's too long for lackluster legacies.

So go forth, plan wisely, and remember: in the grand screenplay of life, make sure their final scene is less "fade to black" and more "standing ovation with fireworks". Because that, dear planners, is how you ensure they're not just remembered, but legendary.

We have a 16-page workbook for you to fill in. We think you may wish to read and pass the book on so please email jenni@blairpublishing.shop and a copy to print will be emailed to you.

Claim Your Free Workbook!

SAMPLE PAGES

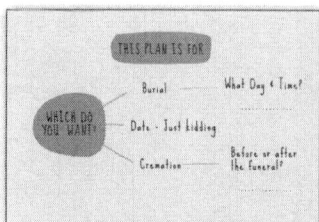
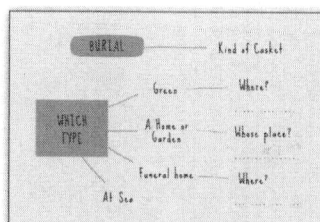
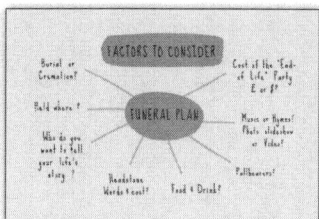
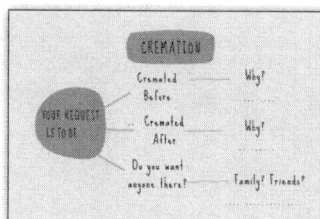

Thank you for purchasing our book!

We would greatly appreciate it if you could share a short review on Amazon! Your feedback truly makes a difference, and we can't wait to hear your thoughts. Thank you for your support!

Kind Regards,
Jenni

Made in the USA
Middletown, DE
24 December 2024

68151135R00044